THE BATTLE

OF BRITAIN

AUGUST-OCTOBER 1940

" The gratitude of every home in our Island, in our Empire, and indeed throughout the world, except in the abodes of the guilty, goes out to the British airmen, who, undaunted by odds, unwearied in their constant challenge and mortal danger, are turning the tide of world war by their prowess and by their devotion. Never in the field of human conflict was so much owed by so many to so few."—THE PRIME MINISTER.

CPP 8101   084795370

THE BATTLE OF BRITAIN

An Air Ministry Account of the Great Days from

8th AUGUST—31st OCTOBER 1940

PUBLISHED BY HIS MAJESTY'S STATIONERY OFFICE, LONDON

The Scene is Set

On Tuesday, 20th August, 1940, at 3.52 in the afternoon, the Prime Minister gave the House of Commons one of those periodic reviews on the progress of the war with which members in particular and the country in general have grown familiar. The occasion was grave. On 8th August, the Germans, after a period of activity against our shipping, which had lasted for somewhat longer than a month, had launched upon this island the first of a series of mass air attacks in daylight. For some ten days, and notably on the 15th and the 18th, men and women in the streets of English towns and villages and in the countryside had seen high up against the background of the summer sky the shift and play of aircraft engaged in the fierce and prolonged combat which has come to be known as the Battle of Britain. The House was crowded. Its mood was one of anxious enthusiasm ; but enthusiasm waxed and anxiety waned as the Prime Minister proceeded to describe the swiftly changing movements of the battle, the opening stages of which some of the members had themselves witnessed.

After referring to the work and achievements of the Navy, Mr. Winston Churchill turned to the war in the air. " The gratitude of every home in our Island," he said, " in our Empire, and indeed throughout the world, except in the abodes of the guilty, goes out to the British airmen, who, undaunted by odds, unwearied in their constant challenge and mortal danger, are turning the tide of world war by their prowess and by their devotion. Never in the field of human conflict was so much owed by so many to so few."

The Prime Minister was speaking at a moment when the battle was still at its height, for it was not until the end of October that the German Luftwaffe virtually abandoned its attacks by daylight and began to rely entirely on a policy of night raiding—its tacit admission of defeat.

It is now possible to tell, in great part, the story of the action on which such high praise had been bestowed. Before doing so, however, it is worth while to recall the extraordinary nature of the battle. Nothing like it has ever been fought before in the history of mankind. It is true that aircraft frequently met in combat in the last war ; but they did so in numbers very small when compared with those which were engaged over the fields of Kent and Sussex, the rolling country of Hampshire and Dorset, the flat lands of Essex and the sprawling mass of London. Moreover, from 1914 to 1918 fights took place either between individual aircraft or between small formations, and an engagement in which more than a hundred aircraft on both sides were involved was rare even in the later stages of the war. The issue was, in fact, decided not in the air, in which element the rival air forces played an important but secondary part, but by slow-moving infantry in the heavy mud of Flanders and the Somme. It may be that the same thing, or something like it, will ultimately happen in the present war. Up to the moment, however, the first decisive encounter between Britain and Germany has taken place in the air and was fought three, four, five, and sometimes more than six miles above the surface of the earth by some hundreds of aircraft flying at speeds often in excess of three hundred miles an hour.

While this great battle was being fought day after day, the men and women of this country went about their business with very little idea of what was happening high up above their heads in the fields of air. This battle was not shrouded in the majestic and terrible smoke of a land bombardment with its roar of guns, its flash of shells, its fountains of erupting earth. There was no sound nor fury—only a pattern of white vapour trails, leisurely changing form and shape, traced by a number of tiny specks scintillating like diamonds in the splendid sunlight.

From very far away there broke out from time to time a chatter against the duller sound of engines. Yet had that chatter not broken out, that remote sound would have changed first to a roar and then to a fierce shriek, punctuated by the crash of heavy bombs as bomber after bomber unloaded its cargo. In a few days the Southern towns of England, the capital of the Empire itself, would have suffered the fate of Warsaw or Rotterdam.

The contest may, indeed, be likened to a duel with rapiers fought by masters of the art of fence. In such an encounter the thrusts and parries are so swift as to be often hard to perceive and the spectator realises that the fight is over only when the loser drops his point or falls defeated to the ground.

THESE WERE THE WEAPONS USED

Before we can understand the general strategy and tactics followed by both sides, something must be said of the weapons used. The Germans sought a decision by sending over five main types of bombers—the Ju. 87, a dive-bomber, the Ju. 88, various types of the Heinkel 111, the Dornier 215 and the Dornier 17. The Ju. 87 type B was a two-seater dive-bomber. It was an all-metal, low-wing cantilever monoplane, armed with two fixed machine-guns, one in each wing, and a movable machine-gun in the aft cockpit. When looked at from straight ahead the wings had the shape of a very flat W. Its maximum speed in level flight was a trifle over 240 miles an hour. The Ju. 88 was also a dive-bomber with a maximum speed of 317 m.p.h. Its crew and armament were similar to those of the Heinkel 111. The Heinkel 111k Mark V. was a low-wing all-metal cantilever monoplane with two engines. It carried a crew of four and was armed with three movable machine-guns, one in the nose, one on the top of the fuselage and one in the stream-lined " blister " underneath. Its maximum speed was nearly 275 m.p.h. The Dornier 215 was a high-wing cantilever monoplane of all-metal construction with three movable machine-guns similarly placed to those of the Heinkel 111k. Its maximum speed was about 312 m.p.h. It was a development of the Dornier 17, familiarly known as " the flying pencil." This aircraft was a mid-wing cantilever monoplane. It was armed with two fixed forward-firing machine-guns in the fuselage, one movable gun in the floor and one on a shielded mounting above the wings. Its maximum speed was about 310 m.p.h. Variations and increases in armament were constantly made in all these aircraft which carried the bombs intended to secure victory. These bombers were protected by fighters of which the Germans used two main types, the Me. 109 and the Me. 110. The Me. 109 in the form then used was a single-seater fighter. It was a low-wing all-metal cantilever monoplane armed with a cannon firing through the airscrew hub, four machine-guns and two more in troughs on the top of the engine cowling. Its maximum speed was a little more than 350 m.p.h. Its pilot was later protected by back and front armour of which the size and shape became standardized during the course of the battle. The Me. 110 was a two-seater fighter powered with two engines. It was an all-metal low-wing cantilever monoplane with two fixed cannons and four fixed machine-guns to fire forward from the nose. It was much larger than the Me. 109 but had not got the same capacity of manœuvre. Its maximum speed did not exceed 365 m.p.h. In this aircraft the crew were protected by back armour only. The Germans also used a few Heinkel 113's. This was a low-wing all-metal cantilever monoplane with a single engine. A cannon fired through the airscrew hub and there were two large-bore machine-guns in the wings. The maximum speed was about 380 m.p.h.

To combat this formidable array of fighters and bombers, which Göring had boasted were " definitely superior " to any British aircraft, the Royal Air Force used the Spitfire, the Hurricane and

Ju. 87 240 M.P.H

Me.109 350 M.P.H.

Me. 110 365 M.P.H.

Ju. 88 317 M.P.H.

He. III K 275 M.P.H.

Do. 215 312 M.P.H.

Do. 17 310 M.P.H.

200 MPH 225 MPH 250 MPH 275 MPH 300 MPH 325 MPH 350 MPH 375 MPH 400 M.

GÖRING'S BOAST: "OUR AIRCRAFT ARE DEFINITELY SUPERIOR"

occasionally the Boulton-Paul Defiant.

The Spitfire Mark I was a single-seater fighter with a Rolls-Royce Merlin engine. It was a low-wing all-metal cantilever monoplane armed with eight Browning machine-guns, four in each wing set to fire forward outside the airscrew disc. The maximum speed was 366 m.p.h. The Hawker Hurricane Mark I. was also a single-seater fighter similarly engined and armed. Its maximum speed was 335 m.p.h. The Hawker Hurricane Mark I. was also a single-seater fighter similarly engined and armed. Its maximum speed was 335 m.p.h. In both these aircraft the pilot was protected by front and back armour. The Boulton-Paul Defiant was a two-seater fighter with a Rolls-Royce engine. It was an all-metal low-wing cantilever monoplane, and was armed with four Browning machine-guns mounted in a power-operated turret.

With such machines as these the Royal Air Force and the Luftwaffe faced each other on 8th August when the battle began.

THE BRITISH FIGHTER FORCE ON GUARD

Before describing it something must first be said about our methods of defence, although it is not easy to do this without giving away "state secrets."

The governing principle is that a sufficient strength of Fighters must be assembled at the required height over a given place where it can intercept the oncoming enemy raid and break it up before it can reach its objective.

There is general agreement that the principle of employing Standing Patrols is impracticable owing to its wastefulness. To keep a sufficient strength of Fighters always in the air to guard our shores from any attack would be beyond the powers of

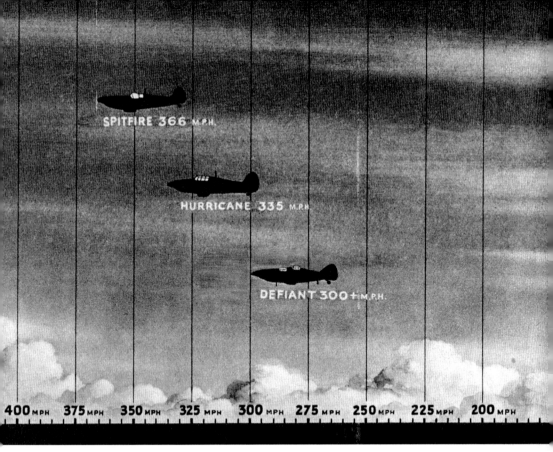

SPITFIRE 366 M.P.H.

HURRICANE 335 M.P.H.

DEFIANT 300+ M.P.H.

400 MPH 375 MPH 350 MPH 325 MPH 300 MPH 275 MPH 250 MPH 225 MPH 200 MPH

BRITAIN'S ANSWER: "'SPITFIRE,' 'HURRICANE,' 'DEFIANT'"

the biggest Air Force imaginable. The Fighter Force is therefore kept on the ground in the interests of economy of effort, and only ordered off the ground when raids appear to be imminent.

Information regarding the approach of the enemy is obtained by a variety of methods and is co-ordinated and passed to "Operations Rooms." The coastline of Britain is divided into Sectors each with its own Fighter Aerodromes and Head-quarters. These Sectors are grouped together under a conveniently situated Group Headquarters which in its turn comes under the general control of Head-quarters, Fighter Command. The in-formation about enemy raids is illustrated by various symbols on a large map table in Group and Sector Operations Rooms, the aim being to give each "Controller" the same picture of the progress of raids in his particular area. In addition to this the

Controllers have all possible information set out before them, such as the location and "state" of their own Squadrons, the weather and cloud conditions all over their area. They are also in touch with Anti-aircraft Defences and Balloon Barrages.

Squadrons are maintained at their Sector Aerodromes at various "states of preparedness." The most relaxed state is "released," which means that the Squadron is not required to operate until a specified hour and that the personnel can be employed in routine maintenance, flying training and instruction, organised games, and that in some cases they may leave the Station. Next comes "Avail-able," which means the Squadrons must prepare to be in the air within so many minutes of receiving the order. "Readi-ness" reduces this to a minimum and is the most advanced state normally used. Occasionally "Stand-by" is employed which means that the pilots are seated in their aircraft, with the engines " off," but all pointing into wind ready to start up, and take off, the moment the leader gets his orders from the Controller.

In good weather conditions and when there is reason to anticipate an attack, Squadrons are perforce kept at a high state of " preparedness " which is relaxed as much as possible when the weather deteriorates. The broad principle is usually to keep one part of the force at " Readiness," a second part at " Advanced Available " and a third at " Normal Available." When the attack develops, the " Readiness " Squadrons are ordered off in appropriate formations and the " Available " Squadrons are ordered to " Readiness " and used as a reserve to meet a second or a third attack or to protect aerodromes or vulnerable points such as aircraft factories.

These orders are issued by the Controller whose function it is to study the Operations Room Map and put a suitable number of aircraft into the air at selected points to intercept the oncoming raids, or to cover vulnerable points. His duty also is to keep a constant watch on his resources so as not to run the risk of being caught by a third or fourth wave of raids, with all his Squadrons on the ground " landed and refuelling." It must be remembered that the endurance of a modern Fighter aircraft, if it is to have ample margin for full throttle work, climbing and fighting, is limited. Allowance must also be made for the journey back to the parent station, especially if visibility is bad.

With the tracks of the enemy raid and of his own Fighters both before his eyes, the Controller's task of making an interception is in theory a comparatively simple mathematical problem. He is in constant touch with his Fighters by radio telephone, is able to give them orders to change course from time to time, so as to put them in the best position for attack.

Once the Fighters report that they have " sighted the enemy," the Controller's task is over, except that he may have to give them a course to bring them back to their aerodromes when the battle is over. The " enemy sighted " signal, the " Tally-ho," is at once transmitted to Group H.Q. and recorded on the Squadron state indicator. The Red Letter day for any Group was on 27th September, when, in No. 11 Group, 21 Squadrons out of 21 ordered up were able to report " enemy sighted." But the successful interception of raids is not always so easy. In practice exercises before the war, thirty per cent. interception was thought satisfactory and fifty per cent. very good. When the test came, however, the percentage rose to seventy-five, ninety, and sometimes a hundred. This consistently high rate of interception made it possible for our superiority in pilots and aircraft to achieve its full effect.

The task of the Controller in setting the stage for the battle is governed by one factor—accurate and timely information about the raids. In clear weather with little or no cloud, the raiders came over at such high altitude that they were almost invisible even with the use of binoculars. The numbers of aircraft employed made a confusion of noise in the high atmosphere and thus increased the difficulty of detecting raids by sound. In cloudy weather this difficulty was increased, for the Observer Corps had then to rely entirely on sound. In view of these difficulties, that Corps and other sources of information deserve very great credit for the remarkably clear, and timely picture of the situation they presented to the Controllers. These, then, set the pieces on the wide chessboard of the English skies and made the opening moves in the contest on the outcome of which the safety of all free peoples depended. Flexibility was their motto. Each day the Controllers held a conference at which every idea or device for thinking and acting one step ahead of their cunning and resourceful foe was set forth, earnestly discussed and, if found useful, adopted. Without this system of central control, no battle, in the proper sense of the word,

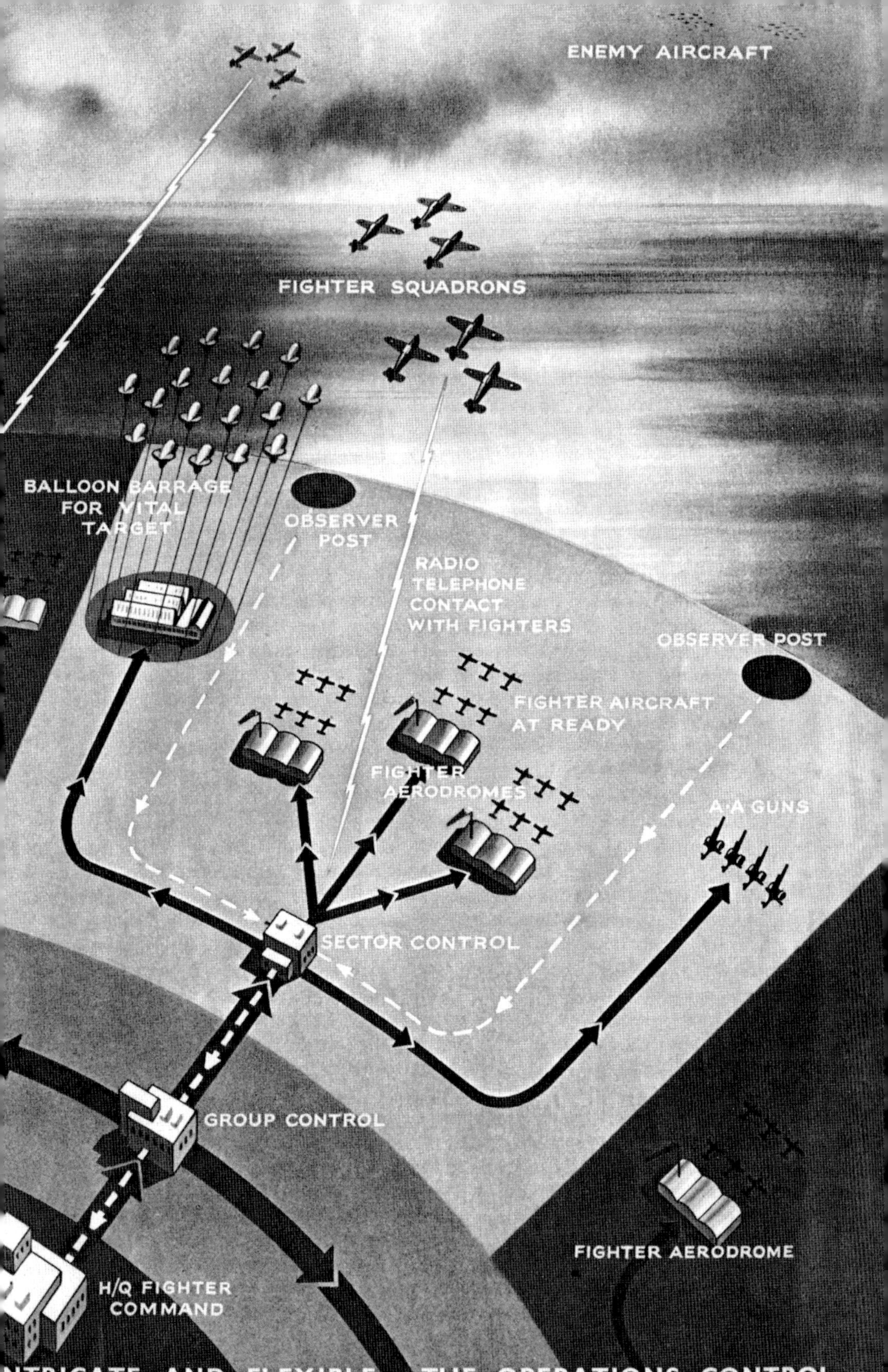

ENEMY AIRCRAFT

FIGHTER SQUADRONS

BALLOON BARRAGE
FOR VITAL
TARGET

OBSERVER
POST

RADIO
TELEPHONE
CONTACT
WITH FIGHTERS

OBSERVER POST

FIGHTER AIRCRAFT
AT READY

FIGHTER
AERODROMES

A·A GUNS

SECTOR CONTROL

GROUP CONTROL

FIGHTER AERODROME

H/Q FIGHTER
COMMAND

NTRICATE AND FLEXIBLE: THE OPERATIONS CONTROL

would have taken place. Squadrons would have gone up haphazard as and when enemy raids were reported. They would either have found themselves heavily outnumbered or with no enemy at all confronting them.

Great care was taken to keep the burden of the fight distributed as equally as possible between all the Squadrons engaged. This was achieved by hard training which continued right through the battle. Whenever there was a lull, new formations were devised and flown, new tactics practised. No Squadron was ever thrown into the fight without previous experience of fighting. They were carefully " nursed " and went into action under the leadership of an experienced squadron leader with many hours of combat to his credit. The importance of team work was fully realised. It was a lesson learnt in France during the battles of May and June, and fortunately many of the pilots who had fought in them were in positions of command during the Battle of Britain. Their knowledge and experience were invaluable.

THE GERMAN COMMAND PLANS A KNOCKOUT

The avowed object of the enemy was to obtain a quick decision and to end the war by the autumn or early winter of 1940. To achieve this an invasion of Britain was evidently thought to be essential. Preparations to launch it were pushed forward with great energy and determination throughout the last days of June, the month of July and the first week of August. By the 8th August the enemy felt himself ready to begin the opening phase, on the success of which his plan depended. Before the German Army could land it was necessary to destroy our coastal convoys, to sink or immobilise such units of the Royal Navy as would dispute its passage, and above all to drive the Royal Air Force from the sky. He, therefore, launched a series of air attacks, first on our shipping and ports and then on our aerodromes. There were four

phases in the battle, the first from 8th –18th August, the second from the 19th August–5th September, the third from the 6th September–5th October, the fourth from the 6th–31st October. During this last phase daylight attacks gave way gradually to night raids which increased as the month went on. It should, however, be remembered that throughout the battle the enemy made use of night as well as day bombing, the first growing in volume and violence as the second fell away.

What was the plan which he sought to carry through in these four phases ? It is impossible to say with certainty at this moment. The German mind is very methodical and immensely painstaking. Schemes are worked out to the last detail ; the organisation is superb and, provided the calculations are correct, the plan goes without a hitch. But again and again history has shown that, if the original plan fails or becomes impracticable, the German has little power of improvisation, and " if the trumpet give an uncertain sound, who shall prepare himself to the battle ? " A brand new plan has to be worked out in full detail, and when this has been done it may well be too late. In this instance the Luftwaffe was designed to prepare the way for the German Army by smashing the enemy's resistance, and it was a fundamental assumption in Berlin that Germany could in every case establish and maintain air supremacy.

The general plan for the use of the Luftwaffe was to seize and exploit the full mastery of the air. This was the main feature in the Polish campaign, in the attacks on Norway and the Low Countries, and even to a large extent in France. Aerodromes were to be put out of action, thus tying the opposing Air Forces to the ground. Ports and communications could then be destroyed without hindrance, the military forces of the enemy paralysed and the German armoured divisions placed in a position to operate undisturbed. Success meant the destruction of civilian morale, and then internal disruption and surrender.

PHASE I

The Offensive is Launched

In the first stage the enemy sent over massed formations of bombers escorted by similar formations of single- and twin-engined fighters. The bombers were for the most part Ju. 87's (dive-bombers), with a smaller quantity of He. 111's, Do. 17's and Ju. 88's. The fighter escorts flew in large, unwieldy formations, from 5,000–10,000 feet above the bombers, where the protection they afforded was not very effective. Using these tactical formations the enemy made twenty-six attacks during this first stage. He began by renewing his assaults on our shipping. It may well be that this was still regarded as the most vulnerable form of target and the easiest to attack, for not only are slow-moving ships difficult to defend, but casualties among the pilots of the defence are always higher when the action is fought over water. He may also have wished to test the strength of our general defences. Success against these would augur well for the next stage. At any rate, on 8th August two convoys were fiercely attacked, one of them twice. Sixty enemy aircraft in the morning and more than a hundred soon after midday, deployed on a front of over twenty miles, tried to sink or disperse a convoy off the Isle of Wight. They succeeded in sinking two ships. In the afternoon at 4.15 more than a hundred and thirty appeared over another convoy off Bournemouth. This they were able to disperse, but they lost fairly heavily in doing so. The enemy renewed the assault three days later, choosing as his targets the towns of Portland and Weymouth, as well as convoys in the Thames Estuary and off Harwich. In these attacks he relied greatly on dive-bombers, which proved no match for our Hurricanes. Nevertheless some damage was done both in Portland and Weymouth. This may have encouraged him, for on 12th August, early in the morning, he launched about two hundred aircraft in eleven waves against Dover. Shortly before noon a hundred and fifty more of the enemy attacked Portsmouth and the Isle of Wight. By this time German losses were already very considerable, for one hundred and eighty-two aircraft had been destroyed.

On the 13th and 15th the attacks on Portsmouth were renewed and in some of them, notably that which began soon after 5 in the afternoon of the 15th, between three and four hundred aircraft were employed. The enemy was by now beginning to realise that our fighter force was considerably stronger than he had imagined. It was evidently time to take drastic action. Our fighters must be put out of commission. Therefore, while still maintaining his attacks on coastal towns, he sent large forces to deal with fighter aerodromes in the South and South-East of England ; Dover, Deal, Hawkinge, Martlesham, Lympne, Middle Wallop, Kenley and Biggin Hill were heavily attacked, some of them many times. A number of the enemy penetrated as far as Croydon.

GERMAN LOSSES RUN INTO HUNDREDS OF AIRCRAFT

Once more the Luftwaffe did a certain amount of damage but at a cost which even Göring must have regarded as excessive. On that day, 15th August, a hundred and eighty German aircraft are known to have been destroyed. Since the opening of the battle he had now lost four hundred and seventy-two aircraft. Nevertheless he still returned to the charge, throwing in between five and six hundred aircraft on 16th August and about the same number on 18th. Rochester, Kenley, Croydon, Biggin Hill, Manston, West Malling, Gosport, Northolt and Tangmere, were the main targets. His losses were again very heavy. In those two days two hundred and forty-five aircraft were shot

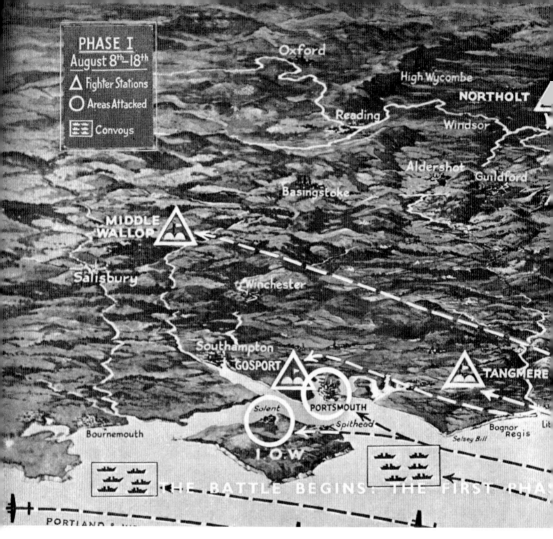

PHASE I
August 8th–18th
△ Fighter Stations
○ Areas Attacked
▭ Convoys

Oxford
High Wycombe
NORTHOLT
Reading
Windsor
Aldershot
Guildford
Basingstoke
MIDDLE WALLOP
Salisbury
Winchester
Southampton
GOSPORT
TANGMERE
Solent
PORTSMOUTH
Spithead
Bognor Regis
Lit
Selsey Bill
Bournemouth
I O W
THE BATTLE BEGINS: THE FIRST PHAS
PORTLAND

down. One of them, a Heinkel III, fell to a Sergeant pilot flying an unarmed Anson aircraft of Training Command. Whether he intentionally rammed the enemy will never be known, for both aircraft fell to the ground interlocked and there were no survivors. On 18th August, in the evening attack on the Thames Estuary, one Squadron alone of thirteen Hurricanes shot down without loss an equal number of the enemy in fifty minutes.

In the ten days since the opening of the attack on 8th August, Göring had now lost six hundred and ninety-seven aircraft. Our own losses during the same period were not light, for we lost one hundred and fifty-three. Sixty pilots were safe though some of them were wounded.

The pace was too hot to last. Göring called halt and gave his Luftwaffe a rest which lasted for five days.

What had he hoped to achieve? An examination of the attacks shows that he began by trying to destroy shipping and ports on the South-East and South Coasts between the North Foreland and Portland. This preliminary test must have shown him the strength of our defences. Nevertheless he proceeded with his plan and next directed his attention to Portland and Portsmouth. Whether these objectives were too tough for him or whether he thought that the four heavy attacks upon them had accomplished his object, he turned away to deliver assaults on fighter and bomber aerodromes mostly near the coast. Throughout this first stage the tactics he followed were usually to open

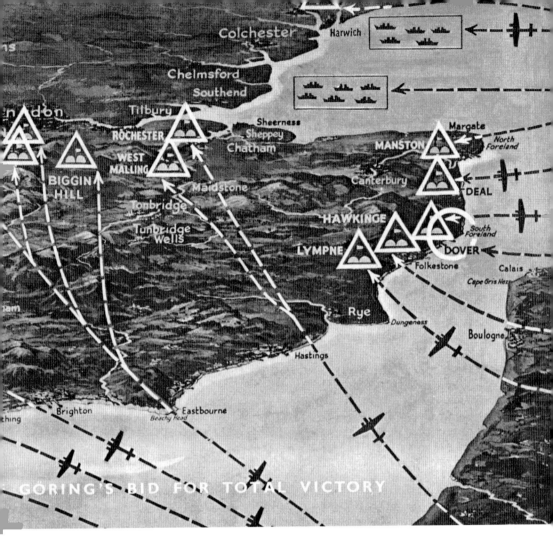

his attack on objectives near the coast in order to draw off our fighters. These feint attacks were followed thirty or forty minutes later by the real attack delivered against ports or aerodromes on the South Coast between Brighton and Portland.

The chief problem created by these tactics was to have a sufficient number of fighters ready to engage the main attack as soon as it could be picked out. Squadrons at the forward aerodromes had to be in instant readiness, but had at the same time to be protected from bombing or machine-gun attacks. Only on one occasion was a Squadron machine-gunned while re-fuelling at a forward aerodrome, and this happened because a protective patrol had not been maintained overhead during the process.

Generally the enemy attacks were countered by using about half the available Squadrons to deal with the enemy fighters and the rest to attack the enemy bombers which flew normally at from 11,000-15,000 feet, descending frequently to 7,000 or 8,000 feet in order to drop their bombs. Our fighter tactics at this stage were to deliver attacks from the stern on the Me. 109's and Me. 110's. This type of attack proved effective because these aircraft were not then armoured. The success of our fighter tactics at this stage can be gauged by a comparison between our losses in pilots and those of the enemy. The ratio was about seven to one and might have been even more striking if so much of the fighting had not taken place over the sea.

PHASE II

The Attack on Inland Aerodromes

Between the end of the first stage and the active beginning of the second there was, as has been said, an interval of five days which were spent by the Germans in widespread reconnaissance by single aircraft, some of which indulged in the spasmodic bombing of aerodromes. These operations cost them thirty-nine aircraft shot down. Our losses were ten aircraft, but six pilots were saved.

During this lull, Göring evidently decided that a change of objectives was necessary. Perhaps he thought that he had achieved the necessary results, and that Portland and Portsmouth together with our coastal aerodromes were virtually out of action. Perhaps he was under the impression that inland aerodromes, factories and other industrial targets would not be as stoutly defended. It is more probable, however, that he merely gave the order for the second part of the plan to be put into operation and disregarded the failure of the first part—either deliberately, or because he had no alternative. In this next stage diversionary attacks against different parts of the country became less frequent. The main attack was now delivered on a wider front. Enemy tactics were also changed. The number of escorting fighters was increased and the size of bomber formations reduced. The covering fighter screen flew at very great heights. Enemy bomber formations were also protected by a box of fighters, some of which flew slightly above to a flank or in rear, others slightly above and ahead, and yet others weaving in and out between the sub-formations of the bombers. This type of formation succeeded on several occasions in breaking through the forward screens of our fighter forces by sheer weight of numbers and in

attaining their objectives even after numerous casualties had been inflicted. On other occasions smallish formations of enemy long-range bombers deliberately left their fighter escort as soon as it had joined battle and proceeded towards South or South-West London unaccompanied. They suffered heavy casualties when engaged by our rear rank of fighters.

Having thus altered his tactical formations the enemy proceeded to deliver some thirty-five major attacks between the 24th August and 5th September. His object, as has been said, was to put out of action inland fighter aerodromes and aircraft factories. He did not, however, disdain purely residential districts in Kent, the Thames Estuary and Essex. These could in no case be described as of military importance.

EIGHT HUNDRED AIRCRAFT ATTACK FIGHTER AERODROMES

From 24th to 29th August he still showed an interest in Portland, Dover and Manston, all of which were heavily attacked. He added other targets as well. Several areas in Essex came in for attention. There was fierce fighting over the North Foreland, Gravesend and Deal. At 6.45 p.m. on the 24th, a hundred and ten German bombers and fighters met a number of our Squadrons in the neighbourhood of Maidstone, but turned and fled before they could be engaged.

The next day he returned to Portsmouth and Southampton where once again he achieved no success, the main attack, delivered at 4 p.m., going astray. A large number of bombs fell into the sea. Heavy assaults were also made in the Dover-Folkestone area, and over the Thames Estuary and in Kent. These continued with a lull of one day until 30th August. On that day and the next the assault was switched to inland fighter aerodromes. Eight hundred aircraft were used in a most determined effort to destroy or temporarily put out of use the aerodromes at Kenley, North Weald, Hornchurch,

Debden, Lympne, Detling, Duxford, Northolt and Biggin Hill.

The opening of September showed little, if any, falling off in the assaults of the enemy. There were three heavy attacks on 1st September, five on 2nd, one on 3rd and two on 4th and 5th. One of the attacks on the 2nd got to within ten miles of London, but most of them were once again directed against fighter aerodromes. This was the last of the thirty-five main attacks delivered in this phase. They cost the Germans five hundred and sixty-two aircraft known to have been destroyed. Our own losses were two hundred and nineteen aircraft, but a hundred and thirty-two of their pilots were saved.

During these twelve days, our own tactical dispositions were altered so as to meet the changed form of attack. The effect of this was to cause the enemy to be met in greater strength and farther away from their inland objectives, while such of his aircraft as were successful in eluding this forward defence were dealt with by Squadrons farther in the rear.

The heavy task of the defence can be realised by the fact that in these first two phases of this great battle from the 8th August to 5th September inclusive, no fewer than 4,523 Fighter Patrols of varying strength in aircraft were flown in daylight, an average of one hundred and fifty-six a day.

HURRICANES AND SPITFIRES
STAY IN THE AIR

What did the enemy succeed in accomplishing in just under a month of heavy fighting during which he flung in squadron after squadron of the Luftwaffe without regard to the cost ? His object, be it remembered, was to " ground " the Fighters of the Royal Air Force and to destroy so large a number of pilots and aircraft as to put

STRONGER SCREENS OF FIGHTERS: SHEER WEIGHT OF NUMBERS

it, temporarily, at least, out of action. As has already been made clear, the Germans, after their opening heavy attacks on convoys and on Portsmouth and Portland, concentrated on fighter aerodromes, first on, or near the coast, and then on those farther inland. Though they had done damage to aerodromes both near the coast and inland and thus put the fighting efficiency of the Fighter Squadrons to considerable strain, they failed entirely to put them out of action. The staff and ground services worked day and night, and the operations of our Fighting Squadrons were not in fact interrupted. By the 6th September the Germans either believed that they had achieved success and that it only remained for them to

bomb a defenceless London until it surrendered, or, following their pre-arranged plan, they automatically switched their attack against the capital because the moment had come to do so.

Those days saw the climax of the first half of the battle. As they drew to a close, Göring's position became not unlike that of Marshal Ney at Waterloo, when at 4.30 in the afternoon he flung thirty-seven squadrons of Kellermann's Cuirassiers, backed by the Heavy Cavalry of the Guard against the hard-pressed British squares. Napoleon was unable to find the necessary support and Ney's effort was made in vain. Göring may perhaps have been in the same position,

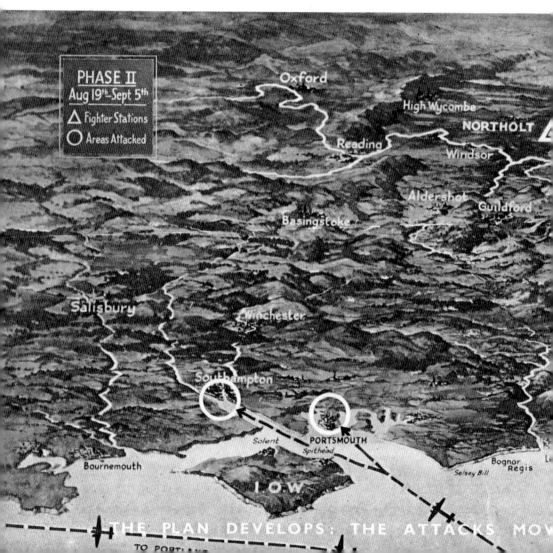

PHASE II
Aug 19th–Sept 5th
△ Fighter Stations
○ Areas Attacked

Oxford
High Wycombe
NORTHOLT
Reading
Windsor
Aldershot
Guildford
Basingstoke
Salisbury
Winchester
Southampton
Bournemouth
Solent
PORTSMOUTH
Spithead
Bognor Regis
Selsey Bill
I.O.W.

THE PLAN DEVELOPS: THE ATTACKS MOV

TO PORTLA

though the attacks of the Luftwaffe continued to be pressed hard throughout September. It may be that Göring had made up his mind to attack targets more easily reached than were our fighter aerodromes. It may be that he was merely working to a time-table. It may be that he thought that our fighter defence was sufficiently weakened. What probably happened can be conveyed by a simple analogy. Imagine a game which involves knocking down a number of objects such as nine-pins or skittles, in so many turns. The player has worked out a detailed scheme for attacking these by stages. The first two or three shots, however, result in misses, and the prudent man would pause to reconsider his policy at

this point. Can he pursue his scheme and still win, or must he abandon it and try another? But this player, Göring, is so certain of winning that he goes on without stopping to think whether or not the preliminary shots have been successful. Suddenly he realises that, with only one or two turns left, he cannot possibly win on the lines of his pre-arranged scheme and he makes a desperate effort to knock down the whole set in the last few shots. This may be no more than a speculation. The facts are that on 7th September Göring switched his attack away from fighter aerodromes on to industrial and other targets, and he began by making London his main objective.

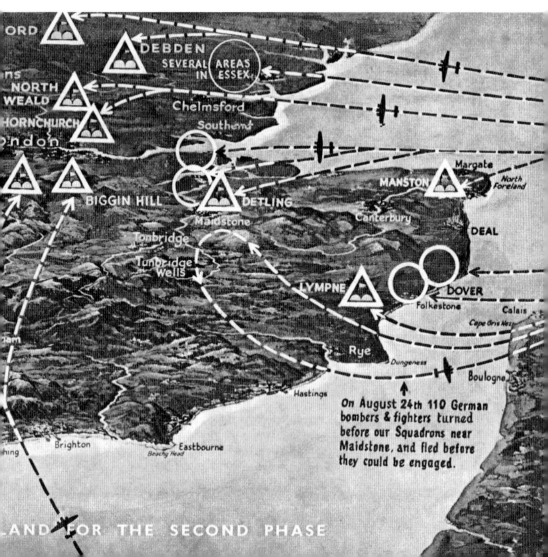

On August 24th 110 German bombers & fighters turned before our Squadrons near Maidstone, and fled before they could be engaged.

...AND FOR THE SECOND PHASE

PHASE III

London versus Göring

The attacks on London on 7th September were made in two or three distinct waves at intervals of about twenty minutes, the whole attack lasting up to an hour. The waves were composed of formations of from twenty to forty bombers with an equal number of fighters in close escort, additional protection being given by large formations of other fighters flying at a much higher altitude. Most of the German aircraft came over at heights above 15,000 feet in sunny skies which made the task of the Observer Corps very difficult.

At this stage, too, the enemy's dive-bombers reappeared in attacks on coastal objectives and shipping off Essex and Kent. They were a diversion for they came over while the mass attacks by the long-range bombers were in progress. By night the Germans greatly increased their attacks by single aircraft. These made no attempt to hit military targets, but contented themselves with dropping their bombs at random over the large area of London.

All the attacks, however, were in essence the same. Over came the German aircraft in one or more of the many formations already described. Somewhere between the coast and London, usually in the Edenbridge-Tunbridge Wells area, but sometimes nearer to the sea, the German squadrons were met by our fighters. The Spitfires tackled the high-flying fighter screen covering the German attack.

The Hurricanes, which had taken off first, engaged the fighter escort, followed by other squadrons who went for the bombers. There were dog-fights all over Kent. The air was for some minutes —never for very long—vibrant with machine-gun fire. People on the ground have described it as like the sound made by a small boy in the next street when he runs a stick along a stretch of iron railings. As a background there was the faint roar of hundreds of engines which on occasion swelled to a fierce note as some crippled enemy fighter or bomber fell to the ground or made for its base dropping lower and lower with Spitfires or Hurricanes diving upon it. Sometimes watchers, like those upon the keep of Hever Castle, would see the blue field of the sky blossom suddenly with the white flowers of parachutes. The warm sun of those superb September days shone on an ever-increasing number of the wrecked carcases of aircraft bearing on their wings the Black Cross of Prussia or the crooked symbol of Nazi power. So numerous were these that, for a period of over a fortnight, more than two battalions of British infantry from the troops stationed in our Southern Marches were required to guard them.

THE LAST THROW

The attack on London and its environs was the crux of the battle. It continued with little respite from the 7th September until 5th October and was the last desperate attempt to win victory. This could no longer be achieved cheaply, for the Luftwaffe had already suffered terrible losses. But it might still be possible to destroy London and thus to win the war. Despite the hard fighting of the previous month the Fighter defences of the R.A.F. were still fighting as hard as ever. They had to be overcome before London could be placed at Hitler's mercy. Göring still believed in superior numbers. These would win the trick. They had brought him swift victory in Poland, Norway, the Low Countries, Belgium and France ; they might still bring victory in Britain. He put forth all his strength in a final endeavour to knock down the nine-pins at any cost. The Luftwaffe delivered thirty-eight major attacks by day between the 6th September and 5th October.

After battering away morning, noon

and night throughout the 6th September against our inland fighter aerodromes, the German Air Force made a tremendous effort on the 7th to reach London and destroy the Docks. Three hundred and fifty bombers and fighters flew in two waves East of Croydon up to the Thames Estuary, some penetrating nearly as far as Cambridge. They were met over Kent and East Surrey, but a number broke through and were engaged over the capital itself. For the first time since that September day in 1666, when Mr. Samuel Pepys informed the King at Whitehall that the City was on fire, Londoners saw flames leaping up from various points in the crowded and densely populated districts of Dockland and Woolwich, while from every German radio station announcers broadcast a running commentary on the action, in which imagination and wishful thinking were nicely blended. London did not emerge unscathed. Damage was inflicted on dock buildings, on several factories, on railway communications, on gas and electricity plants. It was also inflicted on the enemy. One hundred and three German aircraft were destroyed. These heavy casualties shook the German High Command, for though the attacks were renewed and continued, evidently all was no longer well. Still, the Luftwaffe persevered with great tenacity and courage,

delivering heavy attacks on 9th September, using on that occasion a number of four-engined bombers; on the 11th, when about thirty aircraft penetrated to Central London; on the 13th and again on the 15th. Those who got through on the 11th were so savagely handled by our fighter defence that the losses among their crews were estimated to be not fewer than two hundred and fifty. On the next day a single German aircraft penetrated the defence by the clever use of cloud cover and bombed Buckingham Palace in the morning. On the 15th September came the climax; five hundred German aircraft, two hundred and fifty in the morning and two hundred and fifty in the afternoon, fought a running fight with our Hurricanes and Spitfires from Hammersmith to Dungeness, from Bow to the coast of France. This engagement will be described in greater detail later. It cost the enemy one hundred and eighty-five aircraft known to have been destroyed. Altogether, between the 6th September and the 5th October, he had lost eight hundred and eighty-three aircraft.

It is not necessary to record in detail the rest of the fighting which endured to 31st October. Enough has been said to show the nature of the German effort and of our defence. There were, however, three more major assaults delivered on 27th September, 30th September and 5th October.

DAMAGE WAS INFLICTED ON DOCK BUILDINGS . . . AND ON THE ENEMY

Thus between 11th September and 5th October the enemy delivered some thirty-two major attacks by day. In all these, bombers were used and their escort of fighters steadily increased in numbers till the ratio rose to four fighters to one bomber. Of these attacks fifteen were made on the area of Greater London, ten against Kent and the Thames Estuary, six on Southampton and one on Reading. While these last attacks were well executed and pressed home, those on London were less determined than in the opening stages of the battle. On many occasions the enemy jettisoned his bombs before reaching his apparent objective as soon as he found himself in contact with our fighters. Throughout this period the bombing attacks were mostly made from high level. To enable their bombers to reach their targets the Germans sought to draw off our fighter patrols by high altitude rather than by geographical diversions. High fighter screens were sent over to occupy our fighters while the bombers closely escorted by more fighters tried to get through some 6,000 to 10,000 feet below.

SUCCESS OF BRITISH FIGHTER INTERCEPTION

As autumn came on and the sky grew more cloudy, the enemy began to make increasing use of fighters flying very high above the clouds. His most usual practice was to put a very high screen of these fighters

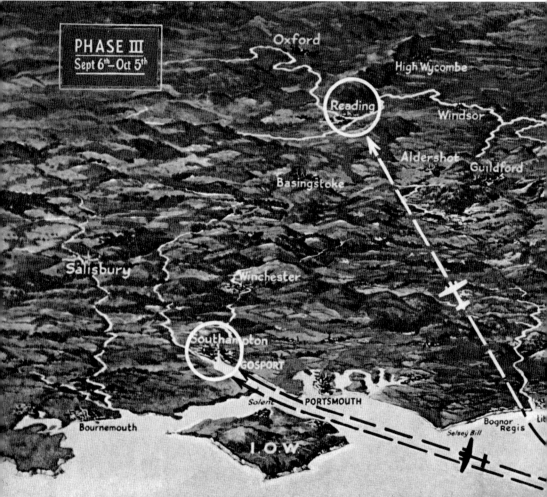

PHASE III
Sept 6th – Oct 5th

SEPTEMBER 1940 · THE CLIMAX · THE WHOLE STRENGT

over Kent from fifteen minutes to three-quarters of an hour before his bombers appeared. The object was evidently to draw off our fighters, exhaust their petrol and thus make it impossible for them to engage the bombers. Sometimes, however, the high-flying enemy fighters appeared only a few minutes before the bombers, which were themselves escorted by other fighters. These escorts were normally divided into two parts, a big formation above and on both flanks or rear of the bombers, and a small formation on the same level as, or slightly in front of, the aircraft they were protecting.

The enemy's high fighter screen was engaged by pairs of Spitfire Squadrons half-way between London and the coast, while wings of two or three Hurricane Squadrons attacked the bombers and their escorts before they reached the fighter aerodromes East and South of London. Other Squadrons formed a third and inner ring patrolling above these aerodromes forming a defensive screen to guard the southern approaches to London. These intercepted the third wave of any attack and mopped up the retreating formations belonging to earlier waves. The success of these tactics may be gauged by the number of casualties inflicted on the Germans. Between 11th September and 5th October, No. 11 Group of Fighter Command alone destroyed four hundred and forty-two enemy aircraft for certain. This was accom-

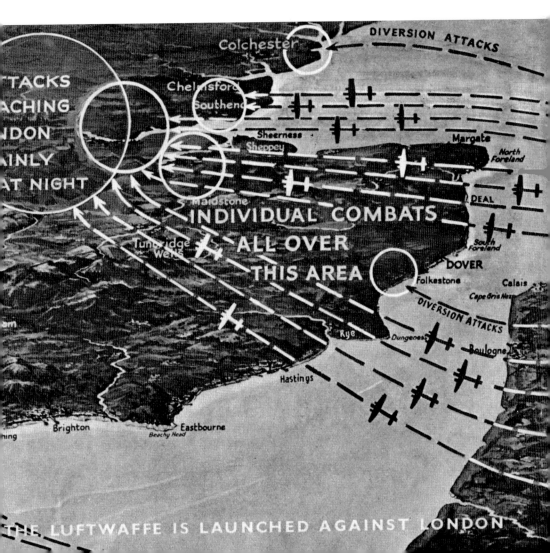

THE LUFTWAFFE IS LAUNCHED AGAINST LONDON

plished with the loss of fifty-eight pilots, giving a ratio of seven and a half enemy to one British pilot lost.

September came and went and by the end of the first week in October our aerodromes had recovered from the damage inflicted on them at the end of August and the beginning of September. The percentage of raids intercepted increased, as did the casualties of the enemy, while our own steadily decreased. Thus on 27th September No. 11 Group destroyed ninety-nine German aircraft, out of a total for the day of one hundred and thirty-three, for the loss of fifteen pilots, a proportion of six and a half to one. Three days later, when thirty-two enemy aircraft were destroyed, the proportion rose to sixteen to one, and on 5th October only one pilot was lost though twenty-two of the enemy were shot down. Many times one aggressively-led squadron was able to break up an enemy bomber formation. On three occasions a lone Hurricane flown by a Sector Commander was successful in causing the enemy to drop his bombs wide of the target. The brunt of all this fighting fell on No. 11 Group. This Group was reinforced when necessary by elements of Numbers 10 and 12 Groups, which were especially useful during the period of the heavy attacks on London.

How hard fought was the battle can be seen from the fact that from 8th September to 5th October inclusive, 3,291 day patrols of varying strengths were flown, and from 6th October to the last day of that month, 2,786, making a total for these fifty-five days of 6,077.

PHASE IV

The Luftwaffe in Retreat

On 6th October, the fourth and final stage of the battle began. The enemy's strategy and method of attack now changed completely. He withdrew nearly all his long-range bombers and tried to achieve his end by means of fighters and fighter-bombers. This change is the surest proof that he had received such a hammering as to make further use of his depleted bombing force by daylight too costly. He preferred to send it over by night, and this he did in increasing numbers. His tactical handling of his fighters and fighter bombers—a few of them were Me. 110's, but they were mostly Me. 109's fitted with a make-shift bomb carrier enabling them to take a pair of bombs at a speed of about three hundred miles an hour—was this.

Mass fighter formations were sent over at a great height in almost continuous waves to attack London, still the principal target. He doubtless hoped by this means to wear out our fighter defence by forcing it to engage, at much higher altitudes, aircraft which were making the best use possible of high cloud cover. In the early stages he reduced the size of his formations and used flights of from two to nine aircraft. The fighter bombers were protected more and more by Me. 110 fighters. Evidently, however, this new plan did not achieve the success for which he hoped, for in the third week of October he reverted once more to large formations flying at 30,000 feet or higher. To enable them to break through, the Germans continued to use the tactics of diversion. Whenever the weather was good enough waves of fighters appeared almost continuously over the South-East of England. Using the cover these provided, very high-flying fighter bombers made frequent and rapid attacks on the London area. On sighting our fighters, however, they often jettisoned their bombs and made off. They showed, in fact, little tendency to engage, but when they did so they sometimes gained the advantage of surprise owing to the height at which they were flying.

THE LAST MOVE COUNTERED

Our own tactics were immediately altered

so successfully that No. 11 Group accounted for one hundred and sixty-seven enemy aircraft in three and a half weeks. The cost to the Group was forty-five pilots. In this phase the number of enemy probably destroyed rose considerably, because the fighting took place so high up that our pilots were unable to see the ultimate fate of many of the German aircraft which fell away after the encounter towards the sea. The physical strain of fighting at heights of 30,000 feet or more proved very severe.

It is possible to detect a feeling of despair in the hearts of the Luftwaffe during this final phase of the struggle. Try as they might, and did, our defences were still not only intact but invulnerable. Occasionally an odd Me. 109 or a small formation broke through and reached London, but the weight of the bombs which they succeeded in dropping was only a fraction of what had been dropped in August and September. Moreover, there was little attempt at precision bombing. There can be no better proof of the enemy's failure than that furnished by the citizens of London. During the early stages, many of them took cover when the sirens sounded. Post Offices, Ministries and Public Departments, large stores —all closed their doors and sent their staffs and any visitors in the building to cover. Very soon, however, it was noticed that most of the noise, at no time to be compared with the nightly barrage which soon became the background of their slumbers, was due to gunfire and not to the explosion of bombs. Trails of white vapour forming fantastic and beautiful patterns in the summer sky were often the only indication that the Luftwaffe was over the capital. These pleased the eye and provided a subject for speculation in the streets and public resorts. Soon, however, even these failed to attract much notice. As the days wore on the Londoner, always confident in the ability of the Royal Air Force to protect him in the hours of daylight, began to take that protection for granted. Except when roof-watchers—the Prime Minister's " Jim Crows "—signalled that danger was imminent, life went on as usual and still does.

There can be no better tribute to the men of the Fighter Squadrons.

NOVEMBER 1940: THE VICTORY WON, LONDON SALUTES THE R.A.F.

15th SEPTEMBER 1940

The Greatest Day

The foregoing is a summary, necessarily brief and incomplete—for the battle took place too recently for a full account to be written—of almost three months of nearly continuous air fighting. The better to comprehend its nature it is necessary to examine in greater detail an individual day's fighting. Sunday, 15th September, is as good a day as any other. It was one of " the great days," as they have come to be called and the actions then fought were described by the Prime Minister in the House of Commons as " the most brilliant and fruitful of any fought upon a large scale up to that date by the fighters of the Royal Air Force." The enemy lost one hundred and eighty-five aircraft. This is what happened.

Over the South-East of England the day of Sunday, 15th September, dawned a little misty, but cleared by eight o'clock and disclosed light cumulus cloud at 2,000 or 3,000 feet. The extent of this cloud varied, and in places it was heavy enough to produce light local showers. Visibility, however, was on the whole good throughout the day ; the slight wind was from the west shifting to north-west as the day advanced.

The first enemy patrols arrived soon after 9 a.m. They were reported to be in the Straits, in the Thames Estuary, off Harwich, and between Lympne and Dungeness. About 11.30 Göring launched the first wave of the morning attack, consisting of a hundred or more aircraft, soon followed by one hundred and fifty more. These crossed the English coast at three main points, near Ramsgate, between Dover and Folkestone and a mile or two north of Dungeness. Their objective was London. This formidable force was composed of Dornier bomber 17's and

215's escorted by Me. 109's. They flew at various heights between 15,000 and 26,000 feet. From the ground the German aircraft looked like black dots at the head of long streamers of white vapour; from the air like specks rapidly growing. They appeared first as model aeroplanes and then, as the range closed, as full-sized aircraft.

Battle was soon joined and raged for about three-quarters of an hour over East Kent and London. Some hundred German bombers burst through our defence and reached the eastern and southern quarters of the capital. A number of them were intercepted above the centre of the city itself just as Big Ben was striking the hour of noon.

To understand the nature of the combat, it must be remembered that the aircraft engaged in it were flying at a speed of between 300 and 400 miles an hour. At that speed place names become almost meaningless. The enemy, for example, might have been intercepted over Maidstone, but not destroyed until within a few miles of Calais. " Place attack was delivered—Hammersmith to Dungeness " or " London to the French Coast." Such phrases in the Intelligence Patrol Reports forcibly illustrate the size of the area over which the battle was fought. That being so, it is better perhaps not to attempt to plot the place of attack too accurately—an almost hopeless task—but to refer to it simply as the Southern Marches of England.

The battle in fact took place roughly in a cube about 80 miles long, 38 broad and from 5 to 6 miles high. It was in this space between noon and half-past that between 150 and 200 individual combats took place. Many of these developed into stern chases which were broken off within a mile or two of the French Coast.

"ACHTUNG, SCHPITFEUER!"

Sixteen Squadrons of No. 11 Group, followed by five from Nos. 10 and 12, were sent up to engage the enemy. All but one of the Squadrons taking part in

the battle were very soon face to face with him. Five Squadrons of Spitfires opened their attack against the oncoming Germans in the Maidstone-Canterbury-Dover-Dungeness area. These were in action slightly before the Hurricane Squadrons, which intercepted farther back, between Maidstone, Tunbridge Wells and South London.

The Germans were found to be flying in various types of formations. The bombers were usually some thousands of feet below the fighters but sometimes this position was reversed. The bombers flew either in Vics (a " V "-shaped formation) of from five to seven aircraft or in lines of five aircraft abreast or in a diamond formation.

The Me. 109's were usually in Vics. One pilot has described the attacking German aircraft as flying in little groups of nine arranged in threes like a sergeant's stripes. Each group of nine was in this case supported by a group of nine Me. 110 fighters with single-seater Me. 109's or He. 113's circling high above.

The enemy soon realised that our defence was awake and active, for the German pilots could be heard calling out to each other over their wireless 'phones " Achtung, Schpitfeuer ! " They had need to keep alert. Our pilots opened fire at an average range of from 250 to 200 yards, closing when necessary to 50. Many of the enemy fighters belonged to the famous Yellow-Nose Squadrons, though some had white noses and even occasionally red.

" JUSTIFICATION FOR OUR NEW TACTICS "

Once the battle was joined, regular formation was frequently lost and each pilot chose an individual foe. The following

THE BOMBERS WERE FOUND

IN VARIOUS FORMATIONS . . .

account of one combat can be taken as typical of the rest.

A pilot, whose Squadron was attacking in echelon starboard, dived out of the sun on to an Me. 109 which blew up after receiving his first burst of fire. By this time he found that another Me. 109 was on his tail. He turned, got it in his sights and set it on fire with several bursts. He was now separated from his comrades and therefore returned to his base. As he was coming down he received a message saying that the enemy were above. He looked up, saw a group of Dorniers at 14,000 feet, climbed and attacked them. He got in a burst at a Dornier ; other friendly fighters came up to help. The enemy aircraft crashed into a wood and exploded.

While the Spitfires and Hurricanes were in action over Kent, other Hurricanes were dealing with such of the enemy as had succeeded by sheer force of numbers in breaking through and reaching the outskirts of London. Fourteen Squadrons of Hurricanes, almost immediately reinforced by three more Squadrons of Spitfires, took up this task, all of them coming into action between noon and twenty past. There ensued a continuous and general engagement extending from London to the coast and beyond.

In it the tactics so carefully thought out, so assiduously practised, secured victory. Let a Squadron Leader describe the results they achieved.

" The 15th of September," he says, " dawned bright and clear at Croydon. It never seemed to do anything else during those exciting weeks of August and September. But to us it was just another day. We weren't interested in Hitler's entry into London ; most of us were wondering whether we should have time to finish breakfast before the first blitz started. We were lucky.

" It wasn't till 9.30 that the sirens started wailing and the order came through to rendezvous base at 20,000 feet. As we were climbing in a southerly direction at 15,000 feet we saw thirty Heinkels supported by fifty Me. 109's 4,000 above them, and twenty No. 110's to a flank, approaching us from above. We turned and climbed, flying in the same direction as the bombers with the whole Squadron stringed out in echelon to port up sun, so that each man had a view of the enemy.

" ' A ' flight timed their attack to perfection, coming down sun in a power dive on the enemy's left flank. As each was selecting his own man, the Me. 110 escort roared in to intercept with cannons blazing at 1,000 yards range, but they were two seconds too late—too late to engage our fighters, but just in time to make them hesitate long enough to miss the bomber leader. Two Heinkels heeled out of the formation.

" Meanwhile the Me. 110's had flashed out of sight, leaving the way clear for ' B ' flight, as long as the Me. 109's stayed above. ' B ' flight leader knew how to bide his time, but just as he was about to launch his attack the Heinkels did the unbelievable thing. They turned south ; into the sun ; and into him. With his first burst the leader destroyed the leading bomber which blew up with such force that it knocked a wing off the left-hand bomber. A little bank and a burst from his guns sent the right-hand Heinkel out of the formation with smoke pouring out of both engines. Before returning home he knocked down an Me. 109. Four aircraft destroyed for an expenditure of 1,200 rounds was the best justification for our new tactics."

DROPPING EVERY FEW MILES

It must be borne in mind that this great battle was made up of Squadron attacks followed by numbers of personal combats, all taking place more or less at the same time over this wide area. Squadrons flying in pairs or wings of three units went into action in formation against an enemy similarly disposed. After the first attack delivered as often as possible out of the sun, they broke up and individual duels took place all over the sky.

Certain of the more striking incidents may be briefly recorded.

There were the dive attacks carried out by one Squadron of Spitfires which twice passed through an enemy bomber formation, each time delivering beam attacks as they did so. These tactics threw the enemy into extreme confusion. The bombers turned almost blindly, it seemed, aircraft dropping in flames or in uncontrolled dives with every few miles of the

return journey. One such aircraft, of which the cowling and cabin top blew off, shed its crew who baled out, all except the rear gunner, who was seen to be hanging from the lower escape hatch until the aircraft dived into a wood, ten miles east of Canterbury.

Then there was the pilot who twice attacked an Me. 109 which each time strove to escape in an almost vertical dive. The first of these from 20,000 feet was successful, for the German pilot straightened out but only to find that the British pilot had followed him down and was close upon him. " By that time," said the British pilot, " I was going faster than the enemy aircraft and I continued firing until I had to pull away to the right to avoid a collision." His burst of fire had taken effect, for the German never recovered, but plunged down until he entered cloud, about 6,000 feet below,

" ACHTUNG, SCHPITFEUER ! "

when the British pilot had to recover from the dive as his aircraft was going at approximately four hundred and eighty miles an hour. " I then made my way through the cloud at a reasonable speed," he reported, " and saw the wreckage of the enemy aircraft burning furiously .... I climbed up through the cloud and narrowly missed colliding with a Ju. 88 which was on fire and being attacked by numerous Hurricanes."

There was also the Dornier which crashed just outside Victoria Station. Members of its crew landed by parachute on the Kennington Oval while the Hurricane pilot who had shot it down and whose aircraft had gone into an uncontrollable spin when the enemy blew up beneath him, landed safely in Chelsea. Nevertheless, the yellow-nosed squadrons, the élite of the German Air Force, acquitted themselves bravely and showed greater skill than their less well-trained comrades. It was observed that they usually attacked in pairs disposed in line astern some seventy-five yards apart.

Occasionally, fire at long range proved effective. Close range combat was the rule, but it is recorded that a Hurricane pilot fired at an enemy aircraft moving faster than his own and about to get out of range, and hit it at 800 yards. This caused it to slow up, and his second burst was fired from 500 yards. Eventually he finished it off at 25 yards. Another Hurricane pilot, who had broken off a fight because the cooling system of the engine of his aircraft was giving trouble, and who was therefore returning to base, encountered a lone Me. 109 which he stalked out of the sun and shot down from 500 yards.

At this stage in the fight it became clear that the enemy bomber pilots felt themselves to be no match for the British. It was generally observed that as soon as contact was established, they jettisoned their bombs then broke formation and turned at once for their base. Thus, twenty Dornier 215's were encountered over the London Docks flying in a diamond formation escorted by Me. 109's " stepped up " to 22,000 feet. The bombers were broken up by a level quarter attack and this enabled our intercepting Squadron to pursue them relentlessly and shoot most of them down.

Occasionally in this confused and struggling fight the British Squadrons found themselves temporarily outnumbering the enemy. Thus at 12.15 a mixed force of Hurricanes and Spitfires amounting to the greater part of five Squadrons was over the south of the Thames, somewhere near Hammersmith. Here they encountered an inferior number of the enemy and did terrible execution.

But it was seldom that we had the advantage in numbers. The enemy, however, seemed unable to profit by his numerical superiority. A single Hurricane, for example, encountered twelve yellow-nosed Messerschmitts flying straight at it. The pilot dived under them but swooped upwards and shot down the rear aircraft from directly underneath. As he still had plenty of speed the British pilot half rolled off the top of his loop and followed the enemy formation which had not apparently perceived the fate of their comrade in the rear rank. The British pilot accordingly destroyed another enemy aircraft from the rear and damaged a second before the Germans became aware of what was happening, and he was forced, being still in the numerical inferiority of nine to one, to break off the action.

The fight was all over by 12.30, and by the time the citizens of London and the South-East of England were sitting down to their Sunday dinner the enemy were in full flight to their bases in Northern France. One of those citizens had special cause to rejoice in the result of the fighting. The Prime Minister had spent the morning in one of the Operations Rooms of No. 11 Group. It was observed that for once his cigar remained unlit as he followed the swift changes of

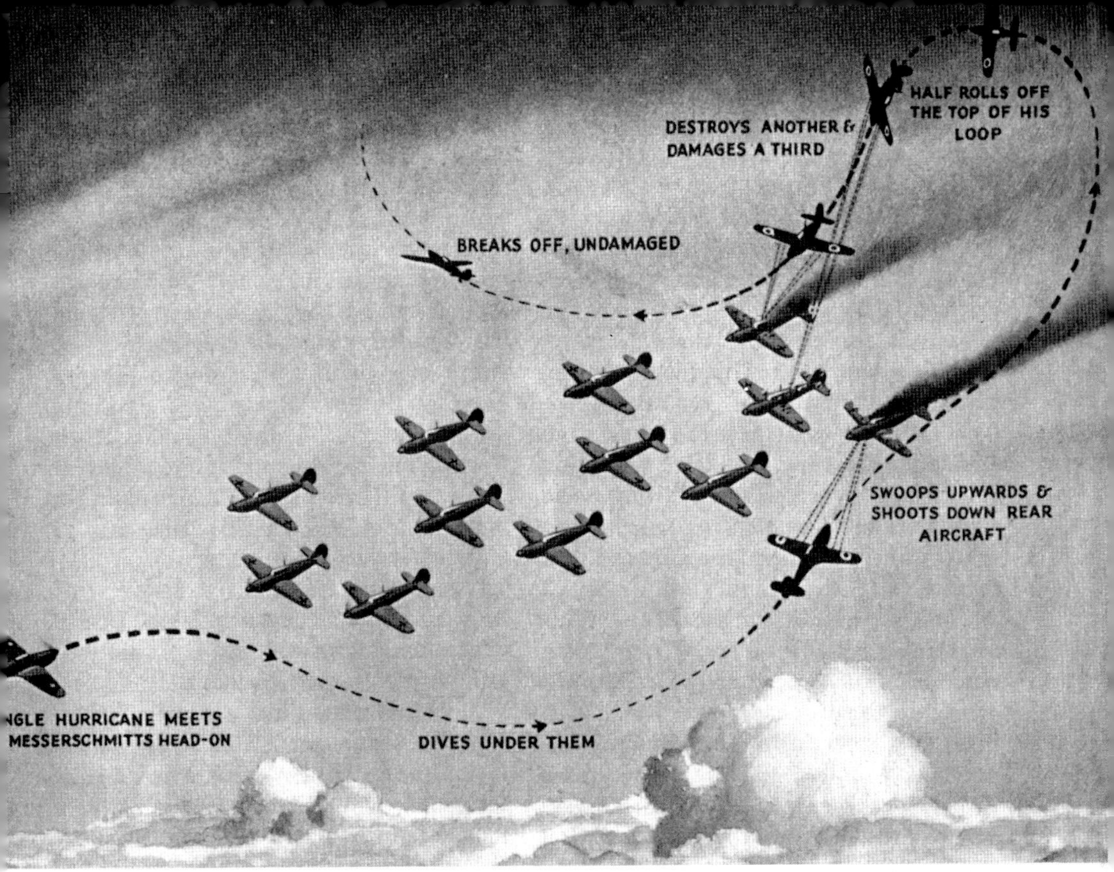
HALF ROLLS OFF THE TOP OF HIS LOOP
DESTROYS ANOTHER & DAMAGES A THIRD
BREAKS OFF, UNDAMAGED
SWOOPS UPWARDS & SHOOTS DOWN REAR AIRCRAFT
NGLE HURRICANE MEETS MESSERSCHMITTS HEAD-ON
DIVES UNDER THEM

ONE INTO TWELVE . . . LEAVES NINE

the battle depicted on the table map before him.

Some of the enemy had for a brief moment succeeded in penetrating into the centre of the capital but they dropped only a few bombs. The fire was too hot, the defence too strong. Seventy of the estimated two hundred and fifty aircraft in the attack, equalling twenty-eight per cent., were seen to crash that morning, ten more were considered probably to have been destroyed and twenty-eight were observed by our pilots to break off action in a damaged condition. These figures, compiled immediately after the fight and in accordance with the very strict rules applied by the Royal Air Force to pilots' reports, probably underestimate the casualties they inflicted. Even so the Luftwaffe lost slightly over forty-three per cent. of the aircraft used in this morning attack.

SECOND WAVE OF AFTERNOON ATTACKERS

Despite the sound and fury of battle that sunny autumn day, the citizens of London had their Sunday dinner in peace. A lull ensued for about an hour and a half. Then, shortly after 2 p.m., fresh enemy forces returned to the attack in about the same strength as had been employed that morning. German aircraft crossed the coast near Dover in two waves, the first of one hundred and fifty, the second of one hundred. These formations spread over the South-East and South-West of Kent and over Maidstone.

Before they could proceed farther they were intercepted by fighters of the Royal Air Force. Twenty-one Squadrons were sent into the air and twenty-one Squadrons made contact with the enemy. This time the numbers on each side were fairly equal, and the fighting superiority of the

British force was immediately established. Our fighters tore into the enemy's formations, ripping through them like a knife through calico. That was how it sounded from the ground. So determined was the British defence, so effective these tactics, that the German formations were again instantly broken up. This was the opportunity for each pilot to single out an adversary, and in a few moments the sky was again a battlefield. In all that space from the Thames Estuary to Dover, from London to the coast, dog-fights were soon in furious progress. Squadrons were swiftly scattered so that two which took off together from their base might, fifteen minutes later, be fighting fifty miles apart.

There was nothing haphazard about this interception of the enemy. It was only possible on such a scale and in so effective a manner because every detail had been planned and tested in the fighting of the previous months. So, as reports came through of the German approach, we were able to despatch from the correct tactical points enough Squadrons to achieve complete interception and the best results, without dissipating our forces. The general principle applied in coping with earlier assaults having proved so successful it was put into effect in this second great attack. Certain Squadrons were detailed to deal with the enemy screen of high-flying fighters halfway between London and the coast. This enabled the others to attack the bomber formations and their close escort before they reached the line of fighter aerodromes East and South of London. Those of the enemy who succeeded in penetrating these defences— some seventy or so—were tackled by Squadrons of Hurricanes, mostly from Nos. 10 and 12 Groups, who came into action over the capital itself. They also pursued stragglers. As in the morning's fighting some two hundred individual combats took place and, although no two were quite alike, the general pattern was the same.

" I engaged the enemy in formation, causing them to scatter in all directions," ran the report of one pilot. " We sighted a strong formation of enemy aircraft," wrote another, " and carried out a head-on attack. The enemy scattered, jettisoned their bombs and turned for home. We encountered heavy cannon fire. . . ." The reports are laconic : " The whole of the nose, including the pilot's cockpit, was shot away. . . ." " I saw tracer flying past my left wing and saw an Me. 109 attack me. . . ." " I saw his perspex burst and the enemy aircraft spun down. . . ." " I did not consider it worth while to waste any more ammunition upon it. . . ." " I then looked for more trouble and saw an He. 111. I attacked and closed to about 10 feet . . ." " I gave him everything I had. . . ." " Aircraft became uncontrollable. I baled out, coming down with left arm paralysed (afterwards learned dislocated). . . "

As in the morning a single British aircraft, in this case a Hurricane, piloted by a Group Captain, encountered a large formation of German aircraft, both fighters and bombers, and went into the attack alone.

" There were," he said on his return, " no other British fighters in sight, so I made a head-on attack on the first section of the bombers, opening at 600 yards and closing to 200 yards." After describing how all alone he broke up the enemy formation the Group Captain adds, " I made further attacks on the retreating bombers, each attack from climbing beam. . . . One Dornier left the formation and lost height. With no ammunition left I could not finish it off. I last saw the bomber at 3,000 feet dropping slowly. . ."

So it appears that each pilot had his own swift decisions to make, his own problems to meet. He was not found wanting. While the fight lasted the Germans were destroyed at the rate of two aircraft a minute. That afternoon's attack cost them ninety-seven destroyed. In the entire day we lost twenty-five aircraft, but fourteen pilots were saved.

Such was a typical day's fighting in a battle which lasted for nearly three months over the South of England.

"Men Like These"

When the order to begin the assault on these islands was given, the morale of the German air crews was undoubtedly high. The reason was obvious. For years these young German airmen had been "groomed" for victory. They were assured of their own superiority as individuals and their omnipotence as a striking force. Had they not seen in the first weeks of the spring of 1940 the terrible predictions of their leader come to pass? Each country Germany had attacked had fallen before the crushing blows of the Nazi war machine, of which they, the Luftwaffe, formed so vital a part. Now, only the British Empire remained inviolate. As those young airmen had swept across Europe from Poland to the English Channel, so they expected to sweep over Britain, subdue her people and prepare the way for an invading army. Disillusion awaited them. As yet, still flushed with victory, they were to see their comrades spin to earth or sea in flames. Nevertheless, let it be said for the German morale, so near it approached to fanaticism, that it never faltered, even when the Luftwaffe was losing seventy, one hundred and one hundred and fifty aircraft during each period of daylight. Certainly the German pilots showed qualities of courage and tenacity; but these were of little avail against the better quality and still higher courage of the British pilots. Even in their hour of defeat some pilots of the Luftwaffe thought that the invasion of Britain might take place at any time and that, if it had to be postponed, it would be successfully accomplished in the spring of 1941. It was not, then, any faltering on their part that caused the daylight attacks to die away.

Of the morale of our own pilots little need be said. The facts are eloquent.

They had only to see the enemy to engage him immediately. Odds were of no account and were cheerfully accepted. Only a very high degree of confidence in their training, in their aircraft and in their leaders could have enabled them to maintain the spirit of aggressive courage which they invariably displayed. That confidence they possessed to the full.

Polish and Czech pilots took their full share in the battle. They possess great qualities of courage and dash. They are truly formidable fighters.

SKY FULL OF SPITFIRES AND HURRICANES

To read the combat reports, written by the pilots immediately after landing from a fight, is to receive the impression of well-trained young men, conscious of their responsibilities and fulfilling them at all times with resolution and high courage.

"Patrolled South of Thames (approximately Gravesend Area) at 25,000 feet," runs the report of one Squadron Leader in action on one of the "great" days. "Saw two squadrons pass underneath us in formation travelling N.W. in purposeful manner. Then saw A.A. bursts,

"THE ENEMY AIRCRAFT SPUN DOWN"

"PORT ENGINE ON FIRE"

so turned Wing and saw enemy aircraft 3,000 feet below to the N.W. Managed perfect approach with two other squadrons between our Hurricanes and sun and enemy aircraft below and down sun. Arrived over enemy aircraft formation of twenty to forty Do. 17's : noticed Me. 109 dive out of sun and warned our Spitfires to look out, Me. 109 broke away and climbed S.E. Was about to attack enemy aircraft which were turning left-handed, i.e., to west and south, when I noticed Spitfires and Hurricanes engaging them. Was compelled to wait for risk of collisions. However, warned wing to watch other friendly fighters and dived down with leading section in formation on to last section of five enemy aircraft. Pilot Officer —— took left-hand Do. 17, I took middle one and Flight Lieutenant —— took the right-hand one which had lost ground on outside of turn. Opened fire at 100 yards in steep dive and saw a large flash behind starboard motor of Dornier as wing caught fire : must have hit petrol pipe or tank; overshot and pulled up steeply. Then carried on and attacked another Do. 17, but had to break away to avoid Spitfire. The sky was then full of Spitfires and Hurricanes queueing up and pushing each other out of the way to get at Dorniers which for once were outnumbered. I squirted at odd Dorniers at close range as they came into my sights,

but could not hold them in my sights for fear of collision with other Spitfires and Hurricanes. Saw collision between Spitfire and Do. 17 which wrecked both aeroplanes. Finally ran out of ammunition chasing crippled and smoking Do. 17 into cloud. It was the finest shambles I've been in, since for once we had position, height and numbers. Enemy aircraft were a dirty looking collection."

Men like these saved England.

Nor must the ground staffs be forgotten. Their tasks were to "service" the fighting aircraft and to maintain communications at any cost. Those attached to the fighter aerodromes, East, South-East and South of London, fitters, mechanics, signallers, telephone operators, despatch riders and the rest carried on under heavy and sustained bombing by day and by night. For the first time since William of Normandy set foot on these shores, men and women of England—the Women's Auxiliary Air Force was in the thick of it—found themselves in the front line. They did not fail and the list of awards they won bears witness to their bravery and their endurance. They made it possible by carrying out their duties, sleep or no sleep, bombs or no bombs, for the Fighter Squadrons to confront the enemy day after day until he was defeated.

Of the anti-aircraft batteries a whole story can be written; but this narrative is concerned only with the part played by the Royal Air Force in the victory. Its controllers received most important aid from the A.A. Units. Their shells bursting in black or white puffs against the sky gave to watchers on the ground or in the air invaluable information concerning the whereabouts of the enemy. Moreover, they accounted for nearly two hundred and fifty hostile aircraft in daylight during the period of the struggle.

SHATTERED AND DISORDERED ARMADA

By 31st October the battle was over. It did not cease dramatically. It died gradually away; but the British victory was none the less certain and complete. Bitter experience had at last taught the enemy the cost of daylight attacks. He took to the cover of night. For what indeed did the Germans accomplish in all their attacks? At the outset they sank five ships and damaged five more sailing in our Coastal convoys; they next did intermittent and sometimes severe damage to aerodromes; they scored hits on a number of factories which caused production to slow down for a short time. In London they did considerable damage to the Docks and to various famous buildings, including Buckingham Palace. They destroyed or damaged beyond repair some thousands of houses; they killed during the day 1,700 persons, nearly all of them civilians, and seriously wounded 3,360. At night 12,581 persons were killed and 16,965 injured. These heavy casualties occurred during the hours when darkness prevented the enemy from being met and turned back as he was in daylight. They provide a striking, if ominous, proof of the efficiency and devotion of the fighters of the Royal Air Force. To what height would those figures have risen had there been no Hurricanes and Spitfires on the alert from dawn to dusk engaging the enemy whenever he appeared—resolute, ruthless, triumphant?

Such, then, was the measure of the enemy's achievement during eighty-four days of almost continuous attack. A little earlier in the year the Germans had taken thirty-seven days to overrun and utterly to cast down the Kingdoms of the Netherlands and of Belgium and the Republic of France. What the Luftwaffe failed to do was to destroy the Fighter Squadrons of the Royal Air Force which were indeed stronger at the end of the battle than at the beginning. This failure meant defeat—defeat of the German Air Force itself, defeat of a carefully designed strategical plan, defeat of that which Hitler most longed for—the invasion of this Island. The Luftwaffe which, as Goebbels said on the eve of the battle, had "prepared the final conquest of the last enemy—England," did its utmost

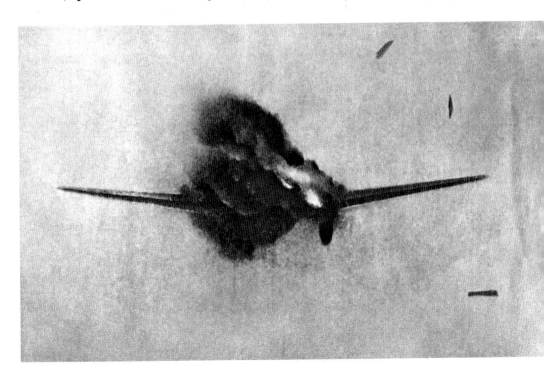

"I GAVE HIM EVERYTHING I HAD"

and paid very heavily for the attempt. Between the 8th August and 31st October, 2,375* German aircraft are known to have been destroyed in daylight. This figure takes no account of those lost at night or those, seen by thousands, staggering back to their French bases, wings and fuselage full of holes, ailerons shot away, engines smoking and dripping glycol, undercarriages dangling—the retreating remnants of a shattered and disordered Armada. This melancholy procession of the defeated was to be observed not once but many times during those summer and autumn days of 1940. Truly it was a great deliverance.

It was not achieved without cost. The Royal Air Force lost 375 pilots killed and

* Throughout this account all figures relating to enemy aircraft concern only those actually destroyed. The number damaged or regarding whose fate complete evidence proved impossible to obtain has not been given.

THE MELANCHOLY REMNANTS OF

358 wounded. This was the price, and of those who died let it be said that :

> " *All the soul*
> *Of man is resolution which expires*
> *Never from valiant men till their last*
> *breath.*"

Such was the Battle of Britain in 1940. Future historians may compare it with Marathon, Trafalgar and the Marne.

Printed by L. T. A. Robinson Ltd. London

ISSUED BY THE MINISTRY OF INFORMATION ON BEHALF
OF THE AIR MINISTRY

First Published 1941.   *Crown Copyright Reserved*

To be purchased directly from His Majesty's Stationery Office at any of the following addresses : York House, Kingsway, London, W.C.2 ;   120, George Street, Edinburgh 2 ;   39-41, King Street, Manchester 2 ; 1, St. Andrew's Crescent, Cardiff ; 80, Chichester Street, Belfast ; or through any bookseller.

Price 6d. net or 20s. for 50 copies.

S.O. Code No. 70-374

HATTERED AND DISORDERED ARMADA